Tap *INTO THE* Mobile Economy

The Appreneur's Guide to Developing

Smartphone and Tablet Apps for Profit

RICH FOREMAN

DANA F. SMITH

EDITED BY: MIDORI YOSHIMURA

DESIGNED BY: SHELLYNN FINSTAD

TABLE OF CONTENTS

TABLE OF CONTENTS

TABLE OF CONTENTS

Rich Foreman and **Dana Smith** have worked together for nearly four years witnessing and participating in the mobile revolution. In 2009 mobile technology was and up and coming technology and smartphones were a luxury. Fast forward four years and we know that mobile technology has disrupted virtually every business and person. We believe mobile applications will be as necessary and common as websites and this industry will continue to grow and evolve. Below is a snapshot of the experience both authors bring to this book.

Apptology CEO, Rich Foreman has 15 years of experience in engineering, mobile application development and account management, spending most of his career in the high tech industry. Rich was instrumental in the product development, customer support and sales management process during his 11 years at WebEx before the $3.2 billion Cisco acquisition. Additionally, Rich is founder of iReadandLearn.com which is a publisher of mobile children's books and educational tools. Rich brings a wealth of experience in the mobile app development industry and he thrives on daily interaction with clients. Rich has a BS in Industrial Engineering from The University of Washington, a Master of Science in Public Administration from Troy State University and was a lieutenant in the Civil Engineer Corps for the US Navy.

Dana Smith has over 15 years of experience in strategy development, product marketing and mobile marketing initiatives working with technology start-ups and Silicon Valley industry leaders. Dana has led the execution of marketing efforts to drive sales traction and results and has extensive experience developing compelling content and initiating high-impact marketing campaigns on a global scale for mobile technology solutions. Dana is a champion of problem solving, brand establishment and go to market plan execution and is a master of creative ideas, collaboration for mutual benefit and relationship building. She holds a dual major with a Bachelor of Arts in Communications and Journalism from California State University, Sacramento.

ACKNOWLEDGMENTS

As a collaborative effort, the authors wish to acknowledge and thank Midori Yoshimura who did a tireless and meticulous job of copy editing. We are enormously grateful and this book would not have been impossible without the creative and enduring efforts of Shellynn Finstad who spent hours on layout, working copy flow, illustrations and graphics. Shellynn is a fantastic designer and she produced the cover which is wonderful – thank you! Inspiration and examples came daily from clients during the idea and development stages of app development so we want to thank Apptology customers as we walked this path together for four years.

INTRODUCTION

[WE ARE LIVING IN THE POST-PC WORLD]

We are living in the post-PC world, where the smartphone has become the dominant means of communication. The ability to run applications, known as apps, on a smartphone has generated its own economy—currently a US$10 billion industry, and projected to grow to a staggering US$155 billion industry in 2017.

Since Apptology first went into business in 2009, I've talked to literally hundreds of people who want to create their own mobile phone app. There are several reasons that people want to develop their own app, which usually include:

- To make money (I'll call these folks appreneurs)
- To promote their own business or cause (app marketers)
- For fun (app hobbyists)

The focus of this book is for the appreneurs out there. This book will serve as a guide to developing your idea into an app and, I hope, allow you to participate in this modern-day Gold Rush.

CHAPTER 1

THE MOBILE REVOLUTION

The fact that you're reading this book means that you already recognize a tremendous opportunity. So, if I don't have to convince you about the importance of mobile technology, you can skip this chapter. Besides, by the time you read this, many of the stats I state will be out of date, and I'm sure all the numbers demonstrating the importance of mobile technology will be significantly higher. You can get more accurate information by simply doing a Google search. But, if you'd like to read more of me stating the obvious, continue on.

THE SMARTPHONE

The first smartphone, defined as a cellular phone with a PDA (personal digital assistant) function, was the IBM Simon Personal Communicator, which debuted in 1992. At the time, it was revolutionary; it sent emails, supported apps, had a touchscreen display and virtual keyboard, and could even handle faxes. IBM did not pursue the next generation of Simon. RIM, Microsoft, and Palm had all been selling some sort of smartphone, but they never captured the imagination of the public. Arguably, the smartphone revolution started when Steve Jobs introduced the iPhone in 2007. He made the smartphone magical.

THE FIRST SMARTPHONE: THE IBM SIMON

Let's take a moment to consider what a smartphone can do:

• **It's a cell phone.** I'm sure that you're already rolling your eyes and saying, "duh," under your breath, but this alone makes it indispensable. Many individuals have done away with landline phones, and only have a cell phone.

- **Text messaging.** For many people (especially those 30 and under), texting has become their primary means of communication (unfortunately, at the expense of proper grammar and conversational skills). Statistically, texts are used more than phone calls to communicate. Texting alone has made smartphones indispensable.

- **Access the Internet**. When cell phones first had Internet access, it was terrible. The connection was unbelievably slow and very expensive. However, access to the Internet via a mobile device has grown dramatically. With long-term evolution (LTE) connections that rival digital subscriber line (DSL) speeds, smartphones are becoming the preferred way to connect to the Internet.

- **Email.** For older folks like myself, and businesses, access to email has become crucial, especially if you're forced away from your desk. The ability to access email on a mobile device has allowed for productivity while away the office.

- **Social media access.** For those that live on Facebook or Twitter, 64 percent access social media sites via a smartphone.

- **GPS.** Global positioning system (GPS) capabilities are now pretty much standard on iPhones. Starting with the iOS 6, the iPhone can now provide turn-by-turn directions (Android has had this feature for some time). This almost negates the need for a dedicated GPS device in your car.

- **Compass.** The iPhone has a built-in digital compass that works like a magnetic needle compass, and is used in conjunction with its GPS capabilities.

- **Multimedia.** Most smartphones can store and play media, both audio and video. The iPhone was initially described as a hybrid iPod and cell phone device.

- **Computer.** Typically, a new smartphone will have a faster processer than a typical three-year-old laptop. The smartphone has essentially become a mobile computer.

- **Camera.** The ability for a smartphone to take both still photographs and video footage has become standard. An interesting side effect is that this capability has been devastating the point-and-shoot camera. Smartphones have become the preferred method for taking casual pictures and videos. This is one of the main reasons that Cisco killed its Flip camcorder without a fight.

- **Voice recorder.** The built-in microphone allows the smartphone to record audio, either as an audio file or as part of a video file.

- **Speech to text.** Most smartphones have speech-to-text functionality. This feature allows the user to convert their speech to text. This is probably one of the most underused features, but it's quite useful once you get the hang of it.

- **Apps.** The ability to run apps that can leverage the smartphones' capabilities sets the stage for infinite possibilities.
- **Low cost.** A high-end smartphone like the Samsung Galaxy or Apple iPhone is typically $200 with a service plan. The lower-end smartphones are often free.

- **Portability.** All the above functionalities, and a smartphone fits in your pocket. Ten years ago, a device like this would have been considered science fiction.

The smartphone has become so essential that, for me, it's one of three items I need to have in my possession when I leave the house (along with my car keys and wallet). As of this writing, there are an estimated 100 million smartphones in the United States, and 800 million worldwide. You can go to your local retail store and buy a "disposable" Android phone for as little as $50 on a pay-as-you-go plan. In many ways, the issue of the digital divide has been solved by the smartphone. I've talked to a few nonprofit organizations that serve the homeless, and have been told that the homeless often carry a smartphone; it has become their connection to the rest of the world.

TABLETS

Tablet devices have been around for some time. The first tablet device was the GRidPad in 1989, which ran MS-DOS and had a stylus. Apple introduced the Newton MessagePad in 1993. Microsoft introduced the Microsoft Tablet PC in 2000. Again, it took Steve Jobs to start another revolution, when he introduced the iPad in 2010.

At first, a tablet device was just a novelty item to me. The iPad was just a big iPhone without the phone. But hey, I could play the games I enjoyed on the iPhone on a bigger screen, and it was nice to watch movies on such a sleek device.

Well, it's become a game changer, with so much more. PC sales have plummeted as tablet device sales have skyrocketed. The technology and market research company Forrester Research estimates that tablet devices will become the primary computing devices by 2016.

THE MOBILE REVOLUTION (STATS)

Anecdotally, if you want to see how prevalent smartphone usage is, take a look around when you're at an airport. I would guess that most people are looking down at their smartphone.

According to Google, the number of Google searches increased by 200 percent in 2012. Forty percent of YouTube views are from a mobile device. Google predicts that a majority of searches will come from a mobile device. Rikard Steiber, Google's global marketing director for mobile and social advertising, stated that Google now considers itself a "mobile first" company.

Other notable tech companies' CEOs that have announced that they are joining the mobile bandwagon include:

- *Mark Zuckerberg,* Facebook's CEO. He stated, "Mobile is absolutely the key and focus for the company."
- *Marissa Mayer,* Yahoo's CEO. She stated that growth strategy is all about mobile, according to a ValueWalk article by Marie Cabural.

I hope that by now, I've convinced you about the importance of mobile technology, and the opportunity that it presents. The next few chapters will discuss how you can foster your ideas and leverage them in a mobile environment to make a profit.

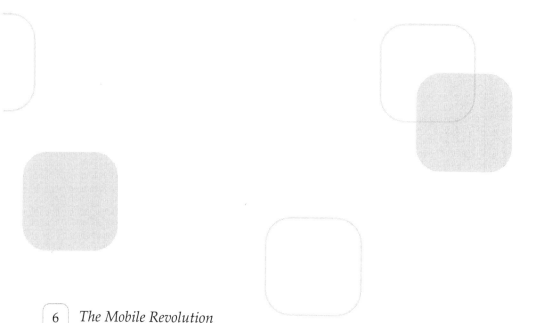

CHAPTER 2

YOUR IDEA: IS THERE AN APP FOR THAT?

"There's an app for that." I love Apple's tagline. It's the concept that apps can do anything. In this chapter, I'll discuss how to foster and develop your app idea.

So, what makes a good idea? If your idea is a game concept, my first comment is that games are very competitive. However, they are very lucrative. Games currently make up the lion's share of the app market. The problem with game apps is that they're also an art. You've got graphic design, sound, gameplay, story, etc. I can't help that much with developing your game concept, but I will talk later about monetization. Personally, I think the ideal app idea is one that solves a business problem for a niche market.

THE IDEAL APP

If you are looking to make a profit on your app, my suggestion is to develop an idea that leverages the power of a smartphone to solve a business problem for a niche market. Why this approach?

Solve a Business Problem

I'm sure that I'm stating the obvious. But if your idea is to be able to solve a business problem, your app has value. This ensures that your app will be used and recommended.

Niche Markets

Niche markets are great because:

1. With hope, if you're developing a solution for a niche market, you're familiar with the field, and hence you would be the ideal person to develop, market, and sell the app.

2. Often, niche markets are underserved in the mobile space, especially if they're not technology related.

3. Marketing is much simpler. To get attention in a niche market, there's probably only one or two trade magazines, professional societies, or annual conferences to which you should reach out.

Case Study: Longshoremen

An example of solving a business problem for a niche market comes from an Apptology client that is a longshoreman. When this client approached me to develop an app for his industry, I was intrigued because longshoremen are not in an industry normally associated with technology. Longshoremen are the dock workers that load and unload cargo from ships.

However, as the client explained his concept, I thought it was brilliant. Longshoremen are union workers, and are required to track their hours daily in a logbook. They literally track their hours in a notebook. The client's idea was to track workers' hours on a mobile device.
As we worked with the client to develop his concept, we added support for iOS and Android, which allowed a larger user base. We also developed a cloud-based database that allowed the app to back up its data on a daily basis. This allowed users to save their data, in the event that their smartphone was lost (or they upgrade). Initially, the client wanted to sell his app at $19.99. However, with the ability to back up data, he switched his pricing to a subscription model and charges 99 cents per month.

So, let's take a look at the market. There are 250,000 longshoremen in the United States. If this client can just capture a 10 percent market share, he will receive a respectable revenue stream.

Research

The first thing you want to do with your idea is to research it. I had a client that spent a considerable amount of time having me sign his nondisclosure agreement (NDA) before talking to me. Once we finally started conversing, I asked him to search for his idea on the App Store, and he quickly found there were over 25 similar apps listed; of course, he quickly lost interest in pursuing his project.

So, for your research, the places you should look into are the various App stores (iOS has the Apple App Store, Android has Google Play andRIM has Blackberry App World, Microsoft has their Microsoft Store. Of course, using the various search engines such as Google and Yahoo is a must. I also encourage you to have a colleague help with your research. It helps to have a second set of eyes.

In terms of feasibility, when you research your idea you should also review the app submission guidelines for the various app stores. The app store guidelines are listed here, beginning with Appendix 3. If you are planning to develop an app on iOS, you really should take the time to review Apple's submission guidelines. They will reject very specific things, like any Russian roulette-type apps, and they can become very vague. Specifically, guideline 10.6 states that they will reject apps that don't meet their high standards. When you talk to a developer, ask them about the feasibility of your app.

Develop Your Idea

In your research, keep in mind that it's not the end of the world if you find another app that does what you're trying to accomplish. You just have to figure out how to make your app better. I always marvel at David-versus-Goliath stories. One of my favorites is how Yahoo was the 800-pound gorilla in the search engine space for years, yet through grassroots marketing was far surpassed by Google.

The next step in this process is to get your idea onto paper (figuratively). I suggest making a mock-up or wireframe, or storyboarding your app idea. I find that when you start storyboarding, more ideas are generated and some ideas are naturally discarded. You can google "iPhone mockup," and find various tools listed. Our Apptology design team uses Keynotopia for our wireframes. To help our clients in developing their idea, I send them a PowerPoint template that they can use to storyboard their concept (see Appendix 7).

After you've created your wireframe, it's a good time to go back to the research mode. For example, if your app is geared for veterinarians, show your wireframe to a few vets and get their feedback. Take what they say and modify your wireframe. (Just remember, you can't make everyone happy, and at some point you'll have to make a judgment call.)

ONCE YOU'VE CREATED YOUR WIREFRAME AND ARE HAPPY WITH IT, THE NEXT STEP IS TO TALK TO A FEW DEVELOPERS

Protecting Your Idea

I get a lot of questions from clients about how they can protect their idea. When talking to developers, you should ask them for a NDA. Or better yet, you may want to have your own NDA. You can get a fairly neutral NDA from LegalZoom for about $15. We have also supplied the text to the NDA that we use for our clients (Appendix 2). The NDA will legally protect your idea from the developer.

If you want to protect your idea from the broader market, that's a little harder, if not impossible. iFart was one of Apple's top 10 paid apps for more than a year, selling millions of downloads. It also spawned numerous copycat apps, so many that Apple announced that they will no longer allow any more fart apps.

The only way that I think you can truly protect your idea is to get a patent. Patents can be granted for business process *(this is the tactic that I suggest you take)*. To get a patent you need to:

1. Conduct a patent search. This is where you conduct research to see if there are any existing patents for your idea. LegalZoom has a cost-effective patent research service. After your research, if you feel that a current patent does not cover your idea, you can move on to the next step.

2. Apply for a provisional patent. A provisional patent essentially declares that you are in the process of applying for a patent. This can be done inexpensively, again via LegalZoom. Once granted, you can display "Patent Pending" on your app.

3. pply for the patent itself. This is the expensive part of the process, in which you have to hire a patent lawyer. This process can cost tens of thousands of dollars.

An example is Uber Technologies, which has a patent pending for booking cabs using a mobile device (I'm summarizing). However, there are already a number of apps that book cabs through a mobile device. I'm not sure if the patent will be granted because of that fact, or what the ramifications for the other cab-booking apps would be if the patent were granted. Also note that even if you have a patent, you have to spend money in court to defend your patent. In the next chapter, I will discuss developing a business plan for your app.

CHAPTER 3

**DEVELOP A
BUSINESS PLAN**

If you plan on making money with your app, you need to develop a business plan. You can google "business plan" for many resources on how to do this. Writing up a business plan forces you to look at your endeavor as a business. Some elements of a business plan should include:

*HOW DO YOU PLAN TO
MARKET AND SELL YOUR APP?*

This is crucial. Just publishing your app on the App Store isn't enough. The game plan from the movie Field of Dreams, "If you build it, they will come," just doesn't apply here. Your app is literally competing with 600,000 other apps. You need to figure out how to market and sell your app.

FINANCIALS

Ultimately, this is the crux of the matter. Does the math make sense? How do you plan to monetize your app? How much capital will you need to develop and market your app, versus how much money will your app generate? The rest of this chapter will focus on figuring out how much it will cost to develop and market your app.

DETERMINING COST

Development

This is typically the first thing that most people look at, in terms of expenses. To be duly diligent, you should get several quotes for how much developing an app will cost. Before you get into this process, I highly recommend you put your idea on paper by creating a wireframe or mock-up (I discussed this in Chapter 2). Having a mock-up will significantly assist developers in creating a quote for you. One place to get multiple good quotes from U.S.-based developers is iPhoneAppQuotes.com. If you are more intrepid and don't mind dealing with offshore developers, you can use Guru.com or Elance.com to get multiple quotes. Of course, you can always google "mobile app developers," and get quotes from the various developers listed. (Shameless plug: you can also visit us at www.apptology.com.)

Before you talk to a developer, if you think you have a great idea that is truly innovative, ask for a NDA. This will prevent your idea from getting Zuckerberged. (If you don't get this reference, see the movie, The Social Network.)

Remember, this exercise is to get an idea of how much it would cost to develop your app. A client of mine revealed that for a project Apptology recently won, the quotes ranged from $7,000 to $50,000. So, how do you handle this huge price range? I would throw out the low bid (they probably didn't understand the scope of your project) and the high bid (they probably throw out a large number just to disqualify you), and go with one of the bids that are clustered together. I would also give more credibility to a developer that took the time to understand your project and ask some good questions.

Marketing

So, how much should you budget for marketing? This is much more nebulous than determining the development cost. A good way to get an idea of marketing costs is to talk to a couple of app marketing agencies like Appency.com or AppMuse.com. They offer several packages that range from a basic evaluation of your app to one that includes a monthly retainer fee. In many cases the cost of marketing an app can be significantly more than the development of the actual app. We will talk specifically about app marketing in Chapter 8.

I hope that after reading this book, you'll look at developing a business plan before you start developing your app. My goal is not to inhibit your idea with analysis paralysis, but to make you consider the various factors that make your app successful.

Monetization Strategy

Making a profit is what monetization boils down to. How are you going to make money? The magic about the app economy is that it has an amazing distribution system. If you were able to make an appearance on the Today show to pitch your app, you could literally get a million downloads the next day and not spend a penny on inventory. Better yet, the funds would magically show up in your account in about 30 days (this example is for Apple's App Store).

So, let's start off with the different ways you can make money with apps.

1. Direct sale of the app. That's the price you charge for the app itself. You can set the price for your app, ranging from free to $999.99. Apple will collect the funds and distribute them to you. Please note that Apple will keep 30 percent of sales.

2. In-app purchase. Within your app, you can allow for purchases of upgrades, additional downloads, subscriptions, virtual items, etc. This also supports a subscription model. You can set the price from $0.99 to $999.99. Again, Apple will keep 30 percent of sales.

3. Ads. There are several ways to generate revenue by having ads within your app.

> • The most common way is to go with a mobile ad provider. The typical model is a pay-per-tap model. There are numerous providers, with Apple iAd and Google AdMob being the dominant players. Appendix 1 provides a list of mobile ad providers.

> • If your app is in a fairly niche space or region, you can create your own ad mechanism and sell ad or sponsorship space yourself.

> • If you are a game developer, kiip.me has an interesting service through which you can reward your player's achievement by providing them with a coupon.

The direct sale approach is the most straightforward method. I recommend this method if your app solves a business problem and you can show a return on investment (ROI).

However, if your app is geared toward the general market, putting a price on it is a barrier for people to download it. For example, the free version of one of our more popular apps had over two million downloads. In contrast, the paid version (which was only 99 cents) had about 2 percent as many downloads as the free version. My recommendation, for general market-type apps, would be a monetization strategy in which the app is a free download. At the time of this writing, if you were to look at the top 10 grossing iPad apps in the Apple App Store, you would see that seven of them are free.

How can a free app be a top grossing app? The answer is in app purchases. Let's dissect today's top grossing app, Clash of the Clans. It's a strategy game in which you can play against other online players. To build your army, you need gems. You can search for gems in the game, or you can accelerate building your army by buying gems. Below is a screenshot of Clash of the Clan's top in-app purchases:

This game is entertaining enough that players have paid $100 for virtual goods. I hope this helps demystify how a free app can generate revenue.

CHAPTER 4   DEVELOPING YOUR APP

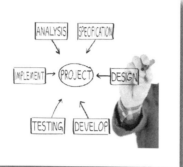

About a fourth of our business is picking up after other developers who left their customers with an incomplete or bug-ridden app. In this chapter, I will talk about factors involved in selecting a developer for your app. Some of the points are obvious; others may give you some food for thought. In the previous chapter, I discussed getting quotes from several developers in order to determine the cost of your app as part of developing your business plan. As a reminder, if you're looking to get a quote from US developers, iPhoneAppQuotes.com is a terrific free resource that promises to provide at least three quotes from US-based developers. Of course, you can always google "mobile app developers" and contact the developers that show up on the search results.

If you don't mind dealing with offshore developers, guru.com, Elance.com, and oDesk.com are good resources. In my conversations with other US-based developers, they tend to stay away from guru.com-type sites because they quickly become commoditized.

Now that you've gathered a few quotes and made contact with a few developers, here are some factors to consider when choosing a developer:

FIXED BID VERSUS HOURLY

My advice based on my experience as a former contracting officer for the US Navy is to go with a developer that will provide a fixed bid for a project, versus an hourly rate. This puts the responsibility on the developer to get you a project for a specific budget. The prerequisite for going with a fixed bid is that the specifications for your project be tight and well defined. If they aren't, the ambiguity will lead to contract modifications that will cost extra money. I've heard of developers that lowball a project and make up the difference with constant contract modifications.

I personally don't recommend going with an hourly rate unless you can manage the workers. You want to make sure that you're paying for development work—not for someone taking a smoking break. The exception to this is if you're working with a developer that you can trust, and the requirements for your project are fluid.

PORTFOLIO

Ask to look at the developer's portfolio. Download their apps. Evaluate their body of work. What you see is probably a good indication of what kind of app the developer can create for you.

REFERENCES

Ask for a list of references from your developer and take the time to contact each one. Recommended questions to ask each reference include:

1. Did the developer have a good process?
2. Was the developer responsive? How was your communication with them?
3. Was the developer helpful with other issues, like setting up an iOS account?
4. How was the quality of their work?

Another great way to check developers' references is to see if they are accredited by the Better Business Bureau (BBB). For example, Apptology's BBB rating is summarized here. If the developer is a BBB member, this also gives you a venue to handle disputes. If the developer wants to keep an 'A' rating with the BBB, they are forced to address your dispute.

WHAT IF YOU GOT HIT BY A BUS?

Ask your developer what would happen if their main developer got hit by a bus. I know it's a strange question, but it's important. I had a client that was developing an app when the developer they were working with just disappeared. He didn't answer any emails or phone calls for a couple of weeks, and the client was forced to find another developer because they were hitting a deadline. It turned out that their developer was arrested for driving under the influence, and had been in jail for a few weeks. So, if you ask the "bus" question, with hope the developer will have some sort of backup plan for you.

CROSS-PLATFORM DEVELOPMENT CAPABILITY

If your business plan has a product road map that includes developing your app on multiple platforms (iOS, Android, RIM, Windows 7, etc.), you should choose a developer that can build applications on multiple platforms. Ideally, they should be able to develop on those platforms, as well as be able to use a cross-platform development tool such as Titanium or appMobi.

THE SOURCE CODE / OWNERSHIP

Two crucial questions to ask your developer are whether they provide the source code at the completion of the project, and if they expect some sort of residual or have some sort of licensing fee. We had a client that approached us, requesting some upgrades to their app because the developer of their app was charging an arm and a leg for the upgrade. Our quote for the project was a fraction of their developer's price. When our client went to our developer to get the source code, they found out that contractually, they did not own the rights to the source code, and were stuck with their developer.

My personal opinion on this matter is that you should have the source code at the end of the project, and own all the rights free and clear after you've paid the developer. As a comparison, if you hire a contractor to build you a house, you expect to own the house free and clear, after you pay the contractor.

The exception I make to this is if the developer is using a template to develop an app for you. By using a template, the developer can build an app for you at a lower price point, and in that case, I think it is acceptable for them to own the source code.

DEVELOPMENT PROCESS

My undergraduate degree was in industrial engineering, so I am a little obsessive about process. That said, when evaluating a developer, ask them about their development process. Some questions to ask your developer include:

1. How and when do you provide feedback?
2. How are scope changes handled?
3. Is there a project manager that you work with?
4. Are there regular project meetings?
5. How is communication handled?
6. What types of project management tools are used?
7. How is quality assurance handled?

I believe that a development process is fundamental for a developer to have, and they should be able to talk about it on the spot. If they can't or you feel that they are winging it, I suggest putting them on the bottom of your list of developers.

TECHNICAL CAPABILITY

This is probably the most crucial factor. Is your developer technically capable of making the app you envisioned? As I stated earlier, a fourth of our business comes from clients that had an app partially built, but their developers weren't technically capable of completing the work. So, how can you tell if a developer is technically capable of developing your app? Some of the factors that I mentioned earlier such as looking at their portfolio, checking their references, and asking about their development processes are good indicators.

But, how do you get beyond the response, "Yeah, yeah, we can do that"? If it's truly a complex app that you're proposing and the developer has invested time in providing a quote, have a follow-up conversation with them and ask how they plan to approach the project, and what the technical challenges are. After speaking with several developers, you should hear some commonalities, and with hope, that will help you flesh out the issues. If one developer brings up a specific point that another didn't, don't be afraid to ask another developer about that same point. Ask lots of questions and take in the education from your conversations with the various developers.

To protect yourself in this category, I recommend that you break up your payment schedule in terms of milestones. For example, it could look like something like this:

Milestone Description	Payment Amount
1 Deposit	One-fourth of project amount
2 Design and acceptance of design	One-fourth of project amount
3 Delivery of alpha build	One-fourth of project amount
4 Delivery and acceptance of app development	One-fourth of project amount

MAINTENANCE PLAN / UPGRADES

All the major platforms upgrade their software roughly once a quarter. Unfortunately, these upgrades may actually break your app. When I first developed my first app, iMotherGoose, Apple had just released iOS 4, and our app was developed on an older software development kit (SDK). To our horror, we found that half the sound files on our app didn't work, and

we had to spend the weekend troubleshooting the problems generated by the upgrade.

So, when choosing a developer, ask them how they handle maintenance. Note that your app should always be evolving. Make sure you also ask them how they handle upgrades.

WARRANTY

Ask your developer if they will agree to a warranty to guarantee their work in writing. So, after the project is delivered and submitted to the various app stores, ask what would happen if a bug were discovered. To be fair, the warranty can only be applied to the specific version of the SDK on which the app was developed. As discussed in the previous section, the developer really can't be responsible for issues caused by an upgrade to the operating system.

PRICING

I saved this key factor for last. I'm not going to go with the cliché that you get what you pay for. I think you can find a high-quality developer that is still cost-effective (shameless plug: like us). I had a client that revealed that the bids for her project ranged from $7,000 to $50,000. Personally, I would throw out the high bid, as I mentioned. I've heard that some vendors just throw out large quotes to weed out their prospects. If there is a bid that is dramatically low, my gut instinct is that they didn't understand the scope of the project. However, before throwing out the vendor's quote, talk to them first, as they may have a template or process that gives them some sort of advantage.

I HOPE THIS GIVES YOU SOME FOOD FOR THOUGHT IN EVALUATING DEVELOPERS FOR YOUR PROJECT

Sample Client Wireframe Files

HOW TO START WIREFRAMING

What does "wireframing" mean? Basically, you're creating a "sketch" of your app's user interface. While many designers jump straight from client meeting to Adobe Photoshop, or even to creating CSS and HTML prototypes, they are missing important opportunities in the design process. Wireframing addresses extremely important issues in strategic design, client adoption, and user-centered design.

Wireframing forces you to think about your user interface design decisions in terms of user needs first, instead of focusing on what looks good.

Blank wireframe screens
provided starting on page 89,
(Appendix 8)

Marketing Your App & Mobile Marketing

Starting to wireframe your app can range from something as simple as sketching layout ideas on a napkin to using more advanced wireframing software, such as OmniGraffle for OS X users or MS Visio for Windows users. Other web-based options include Mockingbird or Balsamiq Mockups.

The important thing is to focus on the strategic *why?* while you create your wireframes, and not on what shade of blue you'll use or what technology you'll use. Usually app designs that have been "wireframed" turn out simpler to design, easier to use and provide invaluable communcation for the development team.

Wireframes are critical components of successful information architecture.

There are two concepts of marketing to discuss here: marketing your mobile app and mobile marketing. Marketing an app is like launching a new business, and requires a plan to be successful. Mobile marketing includes a comprehensive list of marketing tactics, not excluding mobile applications. Both concepts are discussed here, with more emphasis on marketing planning, strategy, and tactics.

MARKETING YOUR APP

As indicated earlier, if you have written a business plan, the marketing plan is a critical component within the plan, and should have identifiable and measurable success metrics associated with it. Outlined here are the components of the marketing plan and what is needed to properly launch and sustain momentum in exposure and/or sales. Whether your app is free or fee-based, understanding your target audience is paramount for success. Listed below are elements of a marketing plan process that you should take into consideration in identifying the tactics that you should employ to achieve the desired results.

Discover | Define | Develop | Deploy | Deliver

DISCOVER

Set Goals:
What will be your measure of success? Goals should be realistic and objectives must be measurable and time-specific. For marketing mobile apps, there are three ways to measure success:

1. *For fee-based apps: direct sales revenue. Remember, the app stores take a percentage of each sale.*

2. *For free apps: add revenue generated through mobile ads integrated within the app.*

3. *For fee-based and free apps: exposure, measured by the number of downloads / popularity / membership / donations, etc.*

Understand Your Target Audience:
Define your audience and get a good understanding of who they are, where they are, their demographics, what media they absorb, and how best to reach them. For example, if you are targeting moms for your app, then define their age group; their children's age group; what media they consume; their income and education levels; where they shop, eat, and play. An understanding of customer behavior and how to influence it need to be incorporated into your marketing plan.

Know Your Competition: What is your competition? Use the Strengths, Weaknesses, Opportunities, and Threats (SWOT) analysis chart to assess your current competitive landscape. It presents information that is important in developing business and marketing plans, and in setting goals and objectives. It tells you where you are and where you need to go in the future.

Some things to consider when determining strengths and weaknesses:

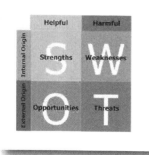

1. Size and financial resources
2. Scale and cost economies
3. Customer perceptions
4. Trends in technology

DEFINE

Now that you have established your goals and objectives, understand your target audience, and are informed about the competitive landscape, you are ready to define the right marketing mix you will need to deploy. Your plan could include a comprehensive, multichannel marketing mix, or may be appropriate for only a handful of programs; this will depend on what the "Discover" phase uncovered. Defining the strategy for each tactic in the complete marketing ecosystem is the next step in the process.

DEVELOP

Once you have defined your marketing tactics and identified the ones that would be the most effective, the next phase is to develop the mechanics of each tactic. This is where the real work begins: planning, producing, and publishing. All marketing initiatives require an individual plan of execution. Outlined below are some of the major tactics to employ, accompanied by checklists, to help you maximize your visibility in marketing your mobile app.

SOCIAL MEDIA

Social Media

Social media is critical for promoting your app. Post updates, comments, news or interesting information on every relevant site, and/or in any associated groups, channels, networks, and forums, as well as on blogs. Create pages/profiles/boards dedicated to your app and its focus, and cover all the major platforms, such as Facebook, Twitter, LinkedIn, YouTube screencasts, Pinterest, Instagram, Google+, etc.

Checklist:

1. Determine which social media platforms are included; strategies may vary with each one.

2. Use key messages and create value propositions and benefit statements.

3. Stay consistent on creative elements across all platforms to establish your brand.

4. Determine and create a schedule of call-to-action programs: contests, surveys, promotions, etc.

5. Keep posts/tweets/comments relevant—covert versus overt.

6. Promote downloads and good reviews.

7. Multimedia content gets noticed…use "dynamic content" such as videos, graphics, and photos.

8. *Associate the app with a cause or a social outreach program.*

9. *In addition to links to the app stores, provide links to relevant stories, articles, and brands that support your sales effort.*

10. *Track your insights and success metrics with each platform.*

PUBLIC RELATIONS AND MEDIA MANAGEMENT

PR Media One key area of marketing is media awareness for your app. There are several vehicles for getting the word out to the appropriate media, and some are free. Business Wire is great, but very expensive. You can get similar exposure through Vocus, PRMac, PRWeb, or PRLog at a lower cost or for free.

Back links are another way to generate coverage. Identify key media within your industry, circle of associations, and networks, and submit the press release online through their website. Most sites actually have a place to do this, and will post your release if it's well written, interesting, and newsworthy for their audience.

Checklist:

1. Create top tier and secondary media lists, with links to editors.

2. Writing a good press release is an art. Make sure your release follows the right format. There are resources online that can help with this. Media alerts are much shorter, have a different format, and are used to update the press/media on news; they're not for major announcements. Make sure your release includes a link to the app store or stores or anywhere your app is available.

3. Write a boilerplate, which is the who, what, when, why, and how of your business or app. This is always at the end of any release or media alert, and should be short and concise.

4. Include photos and videos with your release. Doing so gives it a 40 percent higher chance of getting viewed and read.

5. Send emails directly and personally to key editors, and attach your release with an explanation and personal note. These editors can usually be found online within the site you are targeting.

6. All of the online PR distribution services have metrics and analytics, so check these throughout the day and/or week of your announcement. Read numbers mean just that—someone read your release—while impressions mean that someone has seen your release, but has not necessarily read it.

7. Set Google Alerts with the name of your business or app so that you get daily emails of any postings that occurred.

8. Remember to post any news/publicity that you receive onto all your social networks and your website, and ask your friends, family, and network to re-post it as well.

9. Follow up with editors a week or so after the release and see if they want any more information or if they are interested in an interview for more in-depth coverage.

10. Thank editors for coverage. They will remember you!

EMAIL MARKETING

Email marketing has become very sophisticated, and encompasses many elements when using marketing automation software (MAS). The cost and complexity of these MAS solutions can significantly vary, and should be researched for the best fit and price. Remember that the anti-spam rules apply here too, so any imported database of leads will need to "opt-in" to receive your emails. Companies such as Constant Contact, Vertical Response, and Mail Chimp provide email marketing services with basic functions; the cost will depend on the number of emails sent.

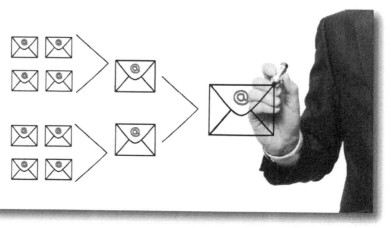

The MAS solutions have multiple layers of capability, and typically include a monthly subscription fee. Their features, which can be custom designed for automation, include customer relationship management (CRM) integration, landing page creations, nurture/drip campaigns, and analytics. Some of the major companies are Marketo, Eloqua, Hubspot, Act-On, Infusionsoft and ExactTarget. Email campaigns through these methods are called inbound marketing because they drive customers to you through a strong call to action that results in a desired outcome. In this case, the action is to promote and download your mobile app.

Checklist:

1. Offer. In addition to promoting your app, provide a piece of content that is of value to entice engagement that is relevant to your application. Examples include white papers, an e-book, a free consultation, coupons, a webinar, demos, etc.

2. Call to action. Provide a link, text, or email to facilitate getting the offer.

3. Lead capture. Have a way to capture the lead through a form that asks for pertinent information that you will want to have for future marketing opportunities.

4. Fulfillment. Once the lead has been secured, fulfill their request with the offer made.

5. Follow-up. Always follow up with a thank you / fulfillment notification to close the loop.

ADVERTISING

PPC Ads

Advertising can be a great way to elevate your position in the app ranking charts, but knowing where, when, and how to create ads can be overwhelming and costly. There are services available from various companies with specific expertise in advertising, but in this area remember to align business goals with budget. Look at mobile ad networks for the best traffic sources and real-time bidding platforms, and consider working with companies that specialize in mobile advertising, such as Google. Pay-per-click advertising on social media sites and key websites is an obvious choice, along with mobile advertising through ad networks. The chart below from Google explains the success rates across media platforms.

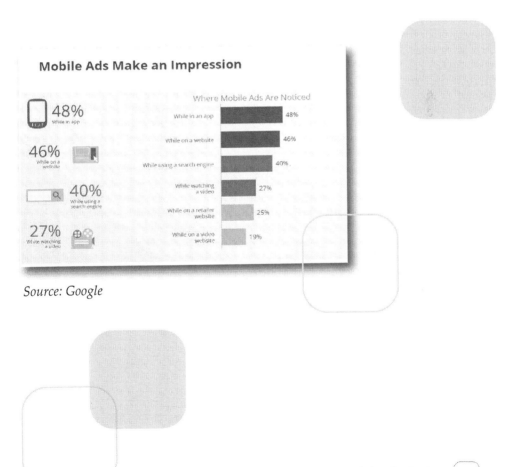

Source: Google

Checklist

1. Use keywords in ad copy for the best search engine optimization (SEO) results.

2. Adapt your ad to a specific audience / industry / media outlet / social site.

3. Define your goals and don't forget the call to action.

4. Try A/B test campaigns for specific time periods to see what works best.

5. Monitor analytics instantly and repeat success tactics

6. A click-through rate (CTR) over 2 percent is good, but not very effective unless you have a very wide reach.

Note: CTR refers to the percentage of visitors that click on an online ad. You divide the number of ad impressions by the number of clicks to get the CTR. For example, if you show an ad 100 times and get two clicks, you have a CTR of 2 percent. According to Google, a reasonable starting goal when buying ads through Google AdWords is 1 percent.

7. Conversion rates refer to the percentage of people who complete the call to action you desire.

8. Drive downloads from organic users in the Apple and Google app stores. A dynamic that exists in mobile app advertising is the relationship between conversions and rank, and the effect both have on generating organic users. This relationship is called organic lift. This is the natural "coattail effect" that conversions have on the acquisition of organic users. There are different ways to track organic lift in the Apple and Android app stores.

In the Apple App Store, ad-driven downloads improve rank, which allows more users to discover your app organically and, in turn, increases organic downloads. Therefore, conversion to organic lift in Apple's App Store is the ratio of organic downloads to ad-driven downloads.

In Google Play, the driver of organic lift is very different than in Apple's App Store. In Google Play, app usage is key to driving organic downloads.

As you acquire new users, use of the app increases. As that usage increases, so does the app's rank within Google Play. This improved ranking is what yields the higher number of organic downloads. The good news for advertisers is that once the app improves its ranking, its position does not degrade the minute an advertiser stops spending. In this way, the advertiser continues to enjoy incremental organic downloads beyond those generated during a campaign.

Source: Fiksu, "Best Practices for Growing your Mobile App Business."

9. Category is critical. Most apps can fit in multiple categories. For example, if your app is a game, does it contain aspects of social networking, music, or entertainment? Rather than defaulting automatically to the "games" category, consider whether your app would be better differentiated in an alternative category.

10. Rankings. Depending on your category, you will set a different optimal rank target. For example, if your app is in a large category, such as games, your objective may be to get into the top 25 apps within that category. Conversely, if your app is in a smaller category, your objective may be to break into the top five. Further complicating this is the fact that some apps get no more organic users at a rank of 15 than 25. So, why pay to be ranked 15th, when there is no difference between organic lift in the 15th position or the 25th? Gain an understanding of your optimal rank, and track performance continuously to ensure that you are not spending more than you need to spend. This will also ensure that your position in the rankings is delivering the required number of users.

VIDEO

Video Rich Media

Video is another critical component that can be used for a variety of purposes. It is rated as the most popular marketing vehicle, and is shared more often than any other medium. Videos were ranked sixth in effectiveness as a marketing tactic, behind social media, newsletters, blogs, case studies, and articles on one's website, but well ahead of many other tactics, according to the study of more than 1,400 business-to-business (B2B) marketing professionals, which was conducted by the Content Marketing Institute.

According to Google, the monthly audience for online video content is steady at around 180 million people. Seventy-six percent of Americans now watch video on mobile devices, 30 percent more than they did a year ago. Video content for promotional, advertising, or educational purposes should be a required component for your digital marketing mix.

There are many companies that specialize in video and rich media production for advertising. If you have the budget, this may be the way to go, but it is certainly not necessary for success.

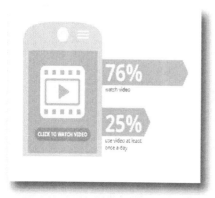

Videos that show the features and functions of your mobile app, or a video case study of usage, go a long way in enticing more people to download your app. And of course, when used in conjunction with social media, the viral impact can be huge!

Source: Google

WEBSITES

Web SEO

Websites are the gateway to lead captures, promotion, exposure, and sales, so improving your SEO should be a top priority. Effective SEO doesn't just help increase your search rankings; it also improves your entire website, from the viewpoint of search engines as well as your visitors. Websites are changing, and it is becoming increasingly important to mobilize the format. Cost of development has decreased, but capability demands are increasing.

Checklist:

1. **Content is king.** The most critical component of your site is content—this is the "why" reason behind people's visits to your site. Good content will be widely read and widely shared by others, often on their own websites, creating vital link-building opportunities. Update your content frequently to focus on the latest information in your niche.

2. **Create a niche.** This may limit your audience, but more importantly minimizes your competition. Become the thought leader in your subject matter, and you will quickly gain a loyal audience and followers.

3. **Keywords.** Use keywords wisely by doing research on the latest trends and information, and employ tools such as Google's Keyword tool. Scatter them strategically throughout your content, your headlines, and your sub-headers.

4. **SEO-friendly URLs.** Make sure that every page of your website has a distinct and search-friendly URL that in a few words describes what the page is about, i.e., http://www.apptology.com/portfolio.

5. **Use meta descriptions and tags.** Create informative, compelling "meta descriptions" of all your webpages. Put the keywords for each page in the search description, using 150-160 characters. A title tag is the main text that

describes an online document. It is the single most important SEO element (behind overall content) on the page, and appears in three key places: the browser, external websites, and the search page results. These should be 70 characters in length, and should offer short descriptions of individual pages they represent, with at least one or two page-relevant keywords within them.

6. **Image attributes.** Images offer excellent SEO-boosting opportunities on Google and other search engines, but it is critical that the photos, graphics, images, etc. have descriptive tags associated with them.

7. **Internal links.** Create a well-organized and thorough link structure within each website page, connecting them to each other through hierarchical text-based hyperlinks.

8. **External links.** Create opportunities for backlinks to your site from other websites so that visitors will be lead back to relevant content on your own website pages. Dedicate time to posting links to social sites, guest post opportunities, articles, blogs, forums, etc., that allow you to publish links back to your website.

9. **Social media sharing.** Install buttons for all the major social sites (Facebook, Twitter, LinkedIn) and other significant platforms on every important page of your website. Readers spread the word, and the content they share can find its way to other websites and lead to backlinks to your website.

10. **Flash and image files.** Search spiders that index websites read only text on websites and are, for the most part, incapable of analyzing Flash or image files, so stay away from both as content mediums. Stick to site-browsing code like jQuery or cascading style sheets (CSS), and create purely text-based written content.
Source: MarketingProfs.com

MOBILE MARKETING

Mobile This encompasses many components and crosses most of the digital marketing mix. The mobile marketing tactics that are outlined here take into consideration that you have marketing functionality built into your mobile application. When customers download your app, it becomes a marketing platform to launch any type of loyalty programs you design into the app.

1. **Text alerts.** These can be sent directly from apps to promote updates, enhancements, events, or any vital information. When people download your app for the first time, they can choose to opt in to these alerts. Keep in mind that anti-spam laws are in effect here, as with email marketing, and it would be a liability risk to send text alerts without approval. Some apps will have customers opt in twice to be sure that they have permission.

2. **Promotions.** Geography-based or location-based coupon offers, mobile check-ins, or limited-time discount specials can also be enabled within some apps, again with opt-in permission. Customers unlock coupons and discounts by "checking in" at your business. These marketing tactics are known as brand loyalty programs because they keep customers engaged, and with hope, will influence buying behaviors by getting customers to purchase products or services. These will vary depending on the type of app or business the app is promoting.

3. **QR codes.** Some apps have a quick response (QR) code scanner built into their functionality. QR codes are a great way to engage customers to link to information, videos, and any other dynamic content. QR codes don't have to be boring black-and-white pixelated boxes anymore. They can be custom branded, with unique logos incorporated in them to make them much more graphically interesting..

4. **E-commerce and m-commerce.** Electronic commerce and mobile commerce are growing exponentially, with m-commerce leading the way. Online or mobile shopping can be another revenue outlet for retailers, and setting up these storefronts is no longer difficult. M-commerce software such as Volusion can easily be integrated as a way to monetize the app.

Here are some m-commerce stats based on a study from Google; these numbers are expected to grow exponentially. They reflect significant ways that mobile technology has changed how consumers are shopping. Sixty-six percent of users have browsed products with the intention of purchasing online, while 40 percent of those who have purchased a product in a physical store have researched it online, up from 33 percent last year.

Source: Google

Overall, the numbers suggest that the trend toward online shopping is continuing, with 36% shopping more online and less at physical retail stores this year. The biggest reason for doing more mobile shopping is convenience, with 44 percent saying this was their biggest motivator.

DEPLOY

This is the ready-set-go! phase of the plan, which means that it's time to pull the switch on all the work that you have defined and developed. Review objectives, incorporate any feedback, make refinements, and launch each program as scheduled.

The marketing budget will most likely be the catalyst that defines which marketing tactics are deployed. However, more money does not necessarily equal more results. This is why the discovery phase is critical, since it will impact how you define each strategy and the desired outcome of these programs, which are all measurable.

DELIVER

This final phase is where you ask if your marketing tactics delivered the results that you defined as goals in the Discover phase. Analyzing success metrics in each tactic should be an ongoing exercise, and course correction should take place along the way. Not all tactics will be successful all the time. Determining the right mix of tools to deploy in this marketing ecosystem for your target audience will be challenging, but also rewarding when successful.

CURRENT MARKETING TRENDS

Personalization

Marketing is moving away from automated batch and blast initiatives to delivering hyper-personalized campaign interactions to win customer loyalty. Capture each of your customers' unique interests and speak to them as individuals, instead of shouting the same message to everyone, hoping it's relevant. Database segmentation is critical here.

Content Curation

Use dynamic content or behavior-driven programs to deliver content that aligns with the customer's preferences, industry, or buying cycle. Recent studies indicate that outbound marketing (paid) has a lower return (2 percent) than inbound marketing (earned) has (10 percent.) Inbound marketing, which provides the customer with content, incentives, and rewards, enticing them seek you out, as opposed to you seeking them out, is far more effective, and creates loyalty. These inbound marketing incentives include white papers, research, educational information, webinars, surveys, reward points or dollars for spending, referrals, and ratings.

Socialites

Social outreach is becoming about the unique interaction and engagement that can take place between you and your customer, and with whomever your customer is sharing your content. Influencing behaviors and brand loyalty through social engagement will continue to be a key tactic for marketers. Customers want an experience, not a transaction.

Shoptimization

This term refers to the shopping experience on mobile platforms, where everything will be available for purchase at your fingertips. Women are the key factor in this trend, and brands will spend more money trying to win and woo women than men.

KEEP LEARNING

The one constant about the mobile space is that it's constantly changing. The iPhone debuted in 2007. iPhone programming was not taught in any colleges. The people that did all the development initially were those that taught themselves, using the iOS SDK.

In general, that's how this app development space is—it's rapidly changing. I've seen one type of app get approved by Apple one month, and the same type of app being rejected the next month. Technology and new features are constantly being rolled out, and you really need to keep up to date on a constant basis.

I subscribe to a couple of daily mobile newsletters, and have several Google Alerts to help keep me current. See Appendix 1 for a list of suggested mobile newsletters.

ANOTHER AVENUE OF REVENUE

In keeping with the theme of rapidly changing environments, another area where there's potential for generating revenue is digital publishing. It's just an afterthought for this book, but in a future update, digital publishing may warrant its own chapter, if not book. The print industry (newspaper, magazines, etc.) has taken a beating in the Internet age. Tablet devices and smartphones may offer a lifeline by providing a new outlet for publishing. If you are able to tap into this market, your publication will have equal billing with Newsweek. Apptology is currently in the beta development stage for a low-cost iPhone/iPad publication solution.

JUST DO IT

If you have an idea for a business, do the research. If you think it's viable, do a basic business plan, follow some of the steps outlined in this book, and just do it. Many people have good ideas. However, most people don't do anything about them, whether because of analysis paralysis or just lack of motivation. The true entrepreneur will run with the ball. Even if the idea is not successful, the education you will gain will be invaluable, and will help you in your next endeavor.

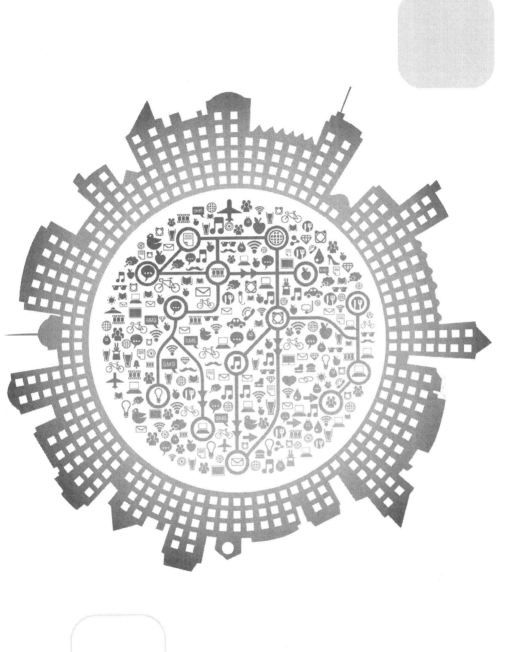

APPENDIX 1.
RESOURCES

APP DEVELOPERS
Apptology.com
Coppermobile.com
Mutualmobile.com

APP MARKETING
Appency.com
AppMuse.com

APP WIREFRAME TOOLS
Balsamiq.com
Keynotopia.com

BUSINESS PLAN
Bplans.com
SBA.gov

FINDING DEVELOPERS
Elance.com
Guru.com
iPhoneAppQuotes.com *(U.S. developers only)*
Odesk.com

LEGAL RESOURCES
LegalShield.com
LegalZoom.com

MOBILE INFORMATION
Appdevelopersalliance.org
Mmaglobal.com
Ourmobileplanet.com

APPENDIX 2.

STANDARD NON-DISCLOSURE AGREEMENT (NDA)

CONFIDENTIALITY AGREEMENT
This Confidentiality Agreement ("Agreement") is made and effective
on_____ (date) by and between

_____

("Owner")

and _____
("Recipient").

1. Confidential Information.

Owner proposes to disclose certain of its confidential and proprietary
information (the "Confidential Information") to Recipient. Confidential
Information shall include all data, materials, products, technology,
computer programs, specifications, manuals, business plans, software,
marketing plans, business plans, financial information, and other
information disclosed or submitted, orally, in writing, or by any other
media, to Recipient by Owner. Confidential Information disclosed orally
shall be identified as such within five (5) days of disclosure.

Nothing herein shall require Owner to disclose any of its information.

2. Recipient's Obligations.

A. Recipient agrees that the Confidential Information is to be considered
confidential and proprietary to Owner and Recipient shall hold the same
in confidence, shall not use the Confidential Information other than for the
purposes of its business with Owner, and shall disclose it only to its

officers, directors, or employees with a specific need to know. Recipient will not disclose, publish or otherwise reveal any of the Confidential Information received from Owner to any other party whatsoever except with the specific prior written authorization of Owner.

B. Confidential Information furnished in tangible form shall not be duplicated by Recipient except for purposes of this Agreement. Upon the request of Owner, Recipient shall return all Confidential Information received in written or tangible form, including copies, or reproductions or other media containing such Confidential Information, within ten (10) days of such request. At Recipient's option, any documents or other media developed by the Recipient containing Confidential Information may be destroyed by Recipient. Recipient shall provide a written certificate to Owner regarding destruction within ten (10) days thereafter.

3. Term.
The obligations of Recipient herein shall be effective

_____(current date)
from the date Owner last discloses any Confidential Information to Recipient pursuant to this Agreement. Further, the obligation not to disclose shall not be affected by bankruptcy, receivership, assignment, attachment or seizure procedures, whether initiated by or against Recipient, nor by the rejection of any agreement between Owner and Recipient, by a trustee of Recipient in bankruptcy, or by the Recipient as a debtor-in-possession or the equivalent of any of the foregoing under local law.

4. Other Information.
Recipient shall have no obligation under this Agreement with respect to Confidential Information which is or becomes publicly available without breach of this Agreement by Recipient; is rightfully received by Recipient without obligations of confidentiality; or is developed by Recipient without

breach of this Agreement; provided, however, such Confidential Information shall not be disclosed until thirty (30) days after written notice of intent to disclose is given to Owner along with the asserted grounds for disclosure.

5. No License.

Nothing contained herein shall be construed as granting or conferring any rights by license or otherwise in any Confidential Information. It is understood and agreed that neither party solicits any change in the organization, business practice, service or products of the other party, and that the disclosure of Confidential Information shall not be construed as evidencing any intent by a party to purchase any products or services of the other party nor as an encouragement to expend funds in development or research efforts. Confidential Information may pertain to prospective or unannounced products. Recipient agrees not to use any Confidential Information as a basis upon which to develop or have a third party develop a competing or similar product.

6. No Publicity.

Recipient agrees not to disclose its participation in this undertaking, the existence or terms and conditions of the Agreement, or the fact that discussions are being held with Owner.

7. Governing Law and Equitable Relief.

This Agreement shall be governed and construed in accordance with the laws of the United States and the State of California and Recipient consents to the exclusive jurisdiction of the state courts and U.S. federal courts located there for any dispute arising out of this Agreement. Recipient agrees that in the event of any breach or threatened breach by Recipient, Owner may obtain, in addition to any other legal remedies which may be available, such equitable relief as may be necessary to protect Owner against any such breach or threatened breach.

8. Final Agreement.

This Agreement terminates and supersedes all prior understandings or agreements on the subject matter hereof. This Agreement may be modified only by a further writing that is duly executed by both parties.

9. No Assignment.

Recipient may not assign this Agreement or any interest herein without Owner's express prior written consent.

10. Severability.

If any term of this Agreement is held by a court of competent jurisdiction to be invalid or unenforceable, then this Agreement, including all of the remaining terms, will remain in full force and effect as if such invalid or unenforceable term had never been included.

11. Notices.

Any notice required by this Agreement or given in connection with it, shall be in writing and shall be given to the appropriate party by personal delivery or by certified mail, postage prepaid, or recognized overnight delivery services.

If to Owner:
If to Recipient:

12. No Implied Waiver.

Either party's failure to insist in any one or more instances upon strict performance by the other party of any of the terms of this Agreement shall not be construed as a waiver of any continuing or subsequent failure to perform or delay in performance of any term hereof.

13. Headings.
Headings used in this Agreement are provided for convenience only and shall not be used to construe meaning or intent.

IN WITNESS WHEREOF, the parties have executed this Agreement as of the date first above written.

Owner:

_____

Recipient:

_____

APPENDIX 3.

APPLE APP STORE REVIEW GUIDELINES

Introduction

We're pleased that you want to invest your talents and time to develop applications for iOS. It has been a rewarding experience - both professionally and financially - for hundreds of thousands of developers and we want to help you join this successful group. We have published our App Store Review Guidelines in the hope that they will help you steer clear of issues as you develop your App and speed you through the approval process when you submit it.

We view Apps different than books or songs, which we do not curate. If you want to criticize a religion, write a book. If you want to describe sex, write a book or a song, or create a medical App. It can get complicated, but we have decided to not allow certain kinds of content in the App Store. It may help to keep some of our broader themes in mind:

• We have lots of kids downloading lots of Apps, and parental controls don't work unless the parents set them up (many don't). So know that we're keeping an eye out for the kids.

• We have over 700,000 Apps in the App Store. If your App doesn't do something useful, unique or provide some form of lasting entertainment, it may not be accepted.

• If your App looks like it was cobbled together in a few days, or you're trying to get your first practice App into the store to impress your friends, please brace yourself for rejection. We have lots of serious developers who don't want their quality Apps to be surrounded by amateur hour.

- We will reject Apps for any content or behavior that we believe is over the line. What line, you ask? Well, as a Supreme Court Justice once said, "I'll know it when I see it". And we think that you will also know it when you cross it.

- If your App is rejected, we have a Review Board that you can appeal to. If you run to the press and trash us, it never helps.

- If you attempt to cheat the system (for example, by trying to trick the review process, steal data from users, copy another developer's work, or manipulate the ratings) your Apps will be removed from the store and you will be expelled from the developer program.

- This is a living document, and new Apps presenting new questions may result in new rules at any time. Perhaps your App will trigger this.

Lastly, we love this stuff too, and honor what you do. We're really trying our best to create the best platform in the world for you to express your talents and make a living too. If it sounds like we're control freaks, well, maybe it's because we're so committed to our users and making sure they have a quality experience with our products. Just like almost all of you are too.

1. Terms and conditions

1.1 As a developer of applications for the App Store you are bound by the terms of the Program License Agreement (PLA), Human Interface Guidelines (HIG), and any other licenses or contracts between you and Apple. The following rules and examples are intended to assist you in gaining acceptance for your App in the App Store, not to amend or remove provisions from any other agreement.

2. Functionality

2.1 Apps that crash will be rejected

2.2 Apps that exhibit bugs will be rejected

2.3 Apps that do not perform as advertised by the developer will be rejected

2.4 Apps that include undocumented or hidden features inconsistent with the description of the App will be rejected

2.5 Apps that use non-public APIs will be rejected

2.6 Apps that read or write data outside its designated container area will be rejected

2.7 Apps that download code in any way or form will be rejected

2.8 Apps that install or launch other executable code will be rejected

2.9 Apps that are "beta", "demo", "trial", or "test" versions will be rejected

2.10 iPhone Apps must also run on iPad without modification, at iPhone resolution, and at 2X iPhone 3GS resolution

2.11 Apps that duplicate Apps already in the App Store may be rejected, particularly if there are many of them, such as fart, burp, flashlight, and Kama Sutra Apps.

2.12 Apps that are not very useful, unique, are simply web sites bundled as Apps, or do not provide any lasting entertainment value may be rejected

2.13 Apps that are primarily marketing materials or advertisements will be rejected

2.14 Apps that are intended to provide trick or fake functionality that are not clearly marked as such will be rejected

2.15 Apps larger than 50MB in size will not download over cellular networks (this is automatically prohibited by the App Store)

2.16 Multitasking Apps may only use background services for their intended purposes: VoIP, audio playback, location, task completion, local notifications, etc.

2.17 Apps that browse the web must use the iOS WebKit framework and WebKit Javascript

2.18 Apps that encourage excessive consumption of alcohol or illegal substances, or encourage minors to consume alcohol or smoke cigarettes, will be rejected

2.19 Apps that provide incorrect diagnostic or other inaccurate device data will be rejected

2.20 Developers "spamming" the App Store with many versions of similar Apps will be removed from the iOS Developer Program

2.21 Apps that are simply a song or movie should be submitted to the iTunes store. Apps that are simply a book should be submitted to the iBookstore.

2.22 Apps that arbitrarily restrict which users may use the App, such as by location or carrier, may be rejected

2.23 Apps must follow the iOS Data Storage Guidelines or they will be rejected

2.24 Apps that are offered in Newsstand must comply with schedules 1, 2 and 3 of the Developer Program License Agreement or they will be rejected

2.25 Apps that display Apps other than your own for purchase or promotion in a manner similar to or confusing with the App Store will be rejected

3. Metadata (name, descriptions, ratings, rankings, etc)

3.1 Apps or metadata that mentions the name of any other mobile platform will be rejected

3.2 Apps with placeholder text will be rejected

3.3 Apps with descriptions not relevant to the application content and functionality will be rejected

3.4 App names in iTunes Connect and as displayed on a device should be similar, so as not to cause confusion

3.5 Small and large App icons should be similar, so as to not to cause confusion

3.6 Apps with App icons and screenshots that do not adhere to the 4+ age rating will be rejected

3.7 Apps with Category and Genre selections that are not appropriate for the App content will be rejected

3.8 Developers are responsible for assigning appropriate ratings to their Apps. Inappropriate ratings may be changed/deleted by Apple

3.9 Developers are responsible for assigning appropriate keywords for their Apps. Inappropriate keywords may be changed/deleted by Apple

3.10 Developers who attempt to manipulate or cheat the user reviews or chart ranking in the App Store with fake or paid reviews, or any other inappropriate methods will be removed from the iOS Developer Program

3.11 Apps which recommend that users restart their iOS device prior to installation or launch may be rejected

3.12 Apps should have all included URLs fully functional when you submit it for review, such as support and privacy policy URLs

4. Location

4.1 Apps that do not notify and obtain user consent before collecting, transmitting, or using location data will be rejected

4.2 Apps that use location-based APIs for automatic or autonomous control of vehicles, aircraft, or other devices will be rejected

4.3 Apps that use location-based APIs for dispatch, fleet management, or emergency services will be rejected

4.4 Location data can only be used when directly relevant to the features and services provided by the App to the user or to support approved advertising uses

5. Push notifications

5.1 Apps that provide Push Notifications without using the Apple Push Notification (APN) API will be rejected

5.2 Apps that use the APN service without obtaining a Push Application ID from Apple will be rejected

5.3 Apps that send Push Notifications without first obtaining user consent will be rejected

5.4 Apps that send sensitive personal or confidential information using Push Notifications will be rejected

5.5 Apps that use Push Notifications to send unsolicited messages, or for the purpose of phishing or spamming will be rejected

5.6 Apps cannot use Push Notifications to send advertising, promotions, or direct marketing of any kind

5.7 Apps cannot charge users for use of Push Notifications

5.8 Apps that excessively use the network capacity or bandwidth of the APN service or unduly burden a device with Push Notifications will be rejected

5.9 Apps that transmit viruses, files, computer code, or programs that may harm or disrupt the normal operation of the APN service will be rejected

6. Game Center

6.1 Apps that display any Player ID to end users or any third party will be rejected

6.2 Apps that use Player IDs for any use other than as approved by the Game Center terms will be rejected

6.3 Developers that attempt to reverse lookup, trace, relate, associate, mine, harvest, or otherwise exploit Player IDs, alias, or other information obtained through the Game Center will be removed from the iOS Developer Program

6.4 Game Center information, such as Leaderboard scores, may only be used in Apps approved for use with the Game Center

6.5 Apps that use Game Center service to send unsolicited messages, or for the purpose of phishing or spamming will be rejected

6.6 Apps that excessively use the network capacity or bandwidth of the Game Center will be rejected

6.7 Apps that transmit viruses, files, computer code, or programs that may harm or disrupt the normal operation of the Game Center service will be rejected

7. Advertising

7.1 Apps that artificially increase the number of impressions or click-throughs of ads will be rejected

7.2 Apps that contain empty iAd banners will be rejected

7.3 Apps that are designed predominantly for the display of ads will be rejected

8. Trademarks and trade dress

8.1 Apps must comply with all terms and conditions explained in the Guidelines for Using Apple Trademarks and Copyrights and the Apple Trademark List

8.2 Apps that suggest or infer that Apple is a source or supplier of the App, or that Apple endorses any particular representation regarding quality or functionality will be rejected

8.3 Apps which appear confusingly similar to an existing Apple product or advertising theme will be rejected

8.4 Apps that misspell Apple product names in their App name (i.e., GPS for Iphone, iTunz) will be rejected

8.5 Apps may not use protected third party material such as trademarks, copyrights, patents or violate 3rd party terms of use. Authorization to use such material must be provided upon request.

9. Media content

9.1 Apps that do not use the MediaPlayer framework to access media in the Music Library will be rejected

9.2 App user interfaces that mimic any iPod interface will be rejected

9.3 Audio streaming content over a cellular network may not use more than 5MB over 5 minutes

9.4 Video streaming content over a cellular network longer than 10 minutes must use HTTP Live Streaming and include a baseline 64 kbps audio-only HTTP Live stream.

10. User interface

10.1 Apps must comply with all terms and conditions explained in the Apple iOS Human Interface Guidelines

10.2 Apps that look similar to Apps bundled on the iPhone, including the App Store, iTunes Store, and iBookstore, will be rejected

10.3 Apps that do not use system provided items, such as buttons and icons, correctly and as described in the Apple iOS Human Interface Guidelines may be rejected

10.4 Apps that create alternate desktop/home screen environments or simulate multi-App widget experiences will be rejected

10.5 Apps that alter the functions of standard switches, such as the Volume Up/Down and Ring/Silent switches, will be rejected

10.6 Apple and our customers place a high value on simple, refined, creative, well thought through interfaces. They take more work but are worth it. Apple sets a high bar. If your user interface is complex or less than very good, it may be rejected

11. Purchasing and currencies

11.1 Apps that unlock or enable additional features or functionality with mechanisms other than the App Store will be rejected

11.2 Apps utilizing a system other than the In-App Purchase API (IAP) to purchase content, functionality, or services in an App will be rejected

11.3 Apps using IAP to purchase physical goods or goods and services used outside of the application will be rejected

11.4 Apps that use IAP to purchase credits or other currencies must consume those credits within the application

11.5 Apps that use IAP to purchase credits or other currencies that expire will be rejected

11.6 Content subscriptions using IAP must last a minimum of 7 days and be available to the user from all of their iOS devices

11.7 Apps that use IAP to purchase items must assign the correct Purchasability type

11.8 Apps that use IAP to purchase access to built-in capabilities provided by iOS, such as the camera or the gyroscope, will be rejected

11.9 Apps containing "rental" content or services that expire after a limited time will be rejected

11.10 Insurance applications must be free, in legal-compliance in the regions distributed, and cannot use IAP

11.11 In general, the more expensive your App, the more thoroughly we will review it

11.12 Apps offering subscriptions must do so using IAP, Apple will share the same 70/30 revenue split with developers for these purchases, as set forth in the Developer Program License Agreement.

11.13 Apps that link to external mechanisms for purchases or subscriptions to be used in the App, such as a "buy" button that goes to a web site to purchase a digital book, will be rejected

11.14 Apps can read or play approved content (specifically magazines, newspapers, books, audio, music, and video) that is subscribed to or purchased outside of the App, as long as there is no button or external link in the App to purchase the approved content. Apple will not receive any portion of the revenues for approved content that is subscribed to or purchased outside of the App

11.15 Apps may only use auto renewing subscriptions for periodicals (newspapers, magazines), business Apps (enterprise, productivity, professional creative, cloud storage) and media Apps (video, audio, voice), or the App will be rejected.

12. Scraping and aggregation

12.1 Applications that scrape any information from Apple sites (for example from apple.com, iTunes Store, App Store, iTunes Connect, Apple Developer Programs, etc) or create rankings using content from Apple sites and services will be rejected

12.2 Applications may use approved Apple RSS feeds such as the iTunes Store RSS feed

12.3 Apps that are simply web clippings, content aggregators, or a collection of links, may be rejected

13. Damage to device

13.1 Apps that encourage users to use an Apple Device in a way that may cause damage to the device will be rejected

13.2 Apps that rapidly drain the device's battery or generate excessive heat will be rejected

14. Personal attacks

14.1 Any App that is defamatory, offensive, mean-spirited, or likely to place the targeted individual or group in harms way will be rejected

14.2 Professional political satirists and humorists are exempt from the ban on offensive or mean-spirited commentary

15. Violence

15.1 Apps portraying realistic images of people or animals being killed or maimed, shot, stabbed, tortured or injured will be rejected

15.2 Apps that depict violence or abuse of children will be rejected

15.3 "Enemies" within the context of a game cannot solely target a specific race, culture, a real government or corporation, or any other real entity
15.4 Apps involving realistic depictions of weapons in such a way as to encourage illegal or reckless use of such weapons will be rejected

15.5 Apps that include games of Russian roulette will be rejected

16. Objectionable content

16.1 Apps that present excessively objectionable or crude content will be rejected

16.2 Apps that are primarily designed to upset or disgust users will be rejected

17. Privacy

17.1 Apps cannot transmit data about a user without obtaining the user's prior permission and providing the user with access to information about how and where the data will be used

17.2 Apps that require users to share personal information, such as email address and date of birth, in order to function will be rejected

17.3 Apps that target minors for data collection will be rejected

18. Pornography

18.1 Apps containing pornographic material, defined by Webster's Dictionary as "explicit descriptions or displays of sexual organs or activities intended to stimulate erotic rather than aesthetic or emotional feelings", will be rejected

18.2 Apps that contain user generated content that is frequently pornographic (ex "Chat Roulette" Apps) will be rejected

19. Religion, culture, and ethnicity

19.1 Apps containing references or commentary about a religious, cultural or ethnic group that are defamatory, offensive, mean-spirited or likely to expose the targeted group to harm or violence will be rejected

19.2 Apps may contain or quote religious text provided the quotes or translations are accurate and not misleading. Commentary should be educational or informative rather than inflammatory

20. Contests, sweepstakes, lotteries, and raffles

20.1 Sweepstakes and contests must be sponsored by the developer/company of the App

20.2 Official rules for sweepstakes and contests, must be presented in the App and make it clear that Apple is not a sponsor or involved in the activity in any manner

20.3 It must be permissible by law for the developer to run a lottery App, and a lottery App must have all of the following characteristics: consideration, chance, and a prize

20.4 Apps that allow a user to directly purchase a lottery or raffle ticket in the App will be rejected

21. Charities and contributions

21.1 Apps that include the ability to make donations to recognized charitable organizations must be free

21.2 The collection of donations must be done via a web site in Safari or an SMS

22. Legal requirements

22.1 Apps must comply with all legal requirements in any location where they are made available to users. It is the developer's obligation to understand and conform to all local laws

22.2 Apps that contain false, fraudulent or misleading representations or use names or icons similar to other Apps will be rejected

22.3 Apps that solicit, promote, or encourage criminal or clearly reckless behavior will be rejected

22.4 Apps that enable illegal file sharing will be rejected

22.5 Apps that are designed for use as illegal gambling aids, including card counters, will be rejected

22.6 Apps that enable anonymous or prank phone calls or SMS/MMS messaging will be rejected

22.7 Developers who create Apps that surreptitiously attempt to discover user passwords or other private user data will be removed from the iOS Developer Program

22.8 Apps which contain DUI checkpoints that are not published by law enforcement agencies, or encourage and enable drunk driving, will be rejected

LIVING DOCUMENT

This document represents our best efforts to share how we review Apps submitted to the App Store, and we hope it is a helpful guide as you develop and submit your Apps. It is a living document that will evolve as we are presented with new Apps and situations, and we'll update it periodically to reflect these changes.

Thank you for developing for iOS. Even though this document is a formidable list of what not to do, please also keep in mind the much shorter list of what you must do. Above all else, join us in trying to surprise and delight users. Show them their world in innovative ways, and let them interact with it like never before. In our experience, users really respond to polish, both in functionality and user interface. Go the extra mile. Give them more than they expect. And take them places where they have never been before. We are ready to help.

Source: © Apple, 2012

APPENDIX 4.

GOOGLE PLAY DEVELOPER PROGRAM POLICIES

The policies listed below play an important role in maintaining a positive experience for everyone using Google Play. Defined terms used here have the same meaning as in the Developer Distribution Agreement. Be sure to check back from time to time, as these policies may change.

Content Policies

Our content policies apply to any content your application displays or links to, including any ads it shows to users and any user-generated content it hosts or links to. In addition to complying with these policies, the content of your app must be rated in accordance with our Content Rating Guidelines.

• Sexually Explicit Material: We don't allow content that contains nudity, graphic sex acts, or sexually explicit material. Google has a zero-tolerance policy against child pornography. If we become aware of content with child pornography, we will report it to the appropriate authorities and delete the Google Accounts of those involved with the distribution.

• Violence and Bullying: Depictions of gratuitous violence are not allowed. Applications should not contain materials that threaten, harass or bully other users.

• Hate Speech: We don't allow the promotion of hatred toward groups of people based on their race or ethnic origin, religion, disability, gender, age, veteran status, or sexual orientation/gender identity.

• Impersonation or Deceptive Behavior: Don't pretend to be someone else, and don't represent that your app is authorized by or produced by another company or organization if that is not the case. Products or the ads they contain also must not mimic functionality or warnings from the operating system or other applications. Developers must not divert users or provide links to any other site that mimics or passes itself off as another application or service. Apps must not have names or icons that appear confusingly similar to existing products, or to apps supplied with the device (such as Camera, Gallery or Messaging).

• Personal and Confidential Information: We don't allow unauthorized publishing or disclosure of people's private and confidential information, such as credit card numbers, Social Security numbers, driver's and other license numbers, or any other information that is not publicly accessible.

• Intellectual Property: Don't infringe on the intellectual property rights of others, (including patent, trademark, trade secret, copyright, and other proprietary rights), or encourage or induce infringement of intellectual property rights. We will respond to clear notices of alleged copyright infringement. For more information or to file a DMCA request, please visit our copyright procedures.

• Illegal Activities: Keep it legal. Don't engage in unlawful activities on this product.

• Gambling: We don't allow content or services that facilitate online gambling, including but not limited to, online casinos, sports betting and lotteries.

• Dangerous Products: Don't transmit viruses, worms, defects, Trojan horses, malware, or any other items that may introduce security vulnerabilities to or harm user devices, applications, or personal data. We don't allow content that harms, interferes with the operation of, or accesses in an unauthorized manner, networks, servers, or other infrastructure.

APPENDIX 4

Apps that collect information (such as the user's location or behavior) without the user's knowledge (spyware), malicious scripts and password phishing scams are also prohibited on Google Play, as are applications that cause users to unknowingly download or install applications from sources outside of Google Play.

NETWORK USAGE AND TERMS

Applications must not create unpredictable network usage that has an adverse impact on a user's service charges or an Authorized Carrier's network. Applications also may not knowingly violate an Authorized Carrier's terms of service for allowed usage or any Google terms of service.

Spam and Placement in the Store
Developers are important partners in maintaining a great user experience on Google Play.

• Do not post repetitive content.

• Product descriptions should not be misleading or loaded with keywords in an attempt to manipulate ranking or relevancy in the Store's search results.

• Developers also should not attempt to change the placement of any Product in the Store by rating an application multiple times, or by offering incentives to users to rate an application with higher or lower ratings.

• Apps that are created by an automated tool or wizard service must not be submitted to Google Play by the operator of that service on behalf of other persons.

- Do not post an app where the primary functionality is to:

   - Drive affiliate traffic to a website or
   - Provide a webview of a website not owned or administered by you (unless you have permission from the website owner/administrator to do so)

- Do not send SMS, email, or other messages on behalf of the user without providing the user with the ability to confirm content and intended recipient.

Paid and Free Applications

- App purchases: Developers charging for applications and downloads from Google Play must do so by using Google Play's payment system.

- In-app purchases: Developers offering additional content, services or functionality within an application downloaded from Google Play must use Google Play's payment system as the method of payment, except:

   - where payment is primarily for physical goods or services (e.g. buying movie tickets; e.g. buying a publication where the price also includes a hard copy subscription); or

   - where payment is for digital content or goods that may be consumed outside of the application itself (e.g. buying songs that can be played on other music players)

Developers must not mislead users about the applications they are selling nor about any in-app services, goods, content or functionality they are selling.

Subscriptions and Cancellations

Google's subscription cancellation policy is that a user will not receive a refund for the current billing period when cancelling a subscription, but will continue to receive issues and updates of the relevant subscription content (if any) for the remainder of the billing period, regardless of the cancellation.

You (as the content or access provider) may implement a more flexible refund policy with your users directly, and it is your responsibility to notify your users of those policies and ensure that the policies comply with applicable law.

AD POLICY

The policy below covers all ads that are implemented in and bundled with apps. These rules are important in maintaining a positive experience for everyone using Android apps from Google Play. Be sure to check back from time to time, as these policies may change.

1. Developer Terms apply to the entire user experience of your application/extension

Please be aware that Google's Developer Distribution Agreement and Developer Program Policies (together, "Developer Terms") apply to each application ("app") as well as any ads or third-party libraries bundled or made available through the app. Offer your users a consistent, policy compliant, and well communicated user experience.

In general, ads are considered part of your app for purposes of content review and compliance with the Developer Terms. Therefore all of the policies, including those concerning illegal activities, violence, sexually explicit content, and privacy violations, apply. Please take care to use advertising which does not violate these policies. Ads which are inconsistent with the app's content rating also violate our Developer Terms.

2. Ads Context

It must be clear to the user which app each ad is associated with or implemented in. Ads must not make changes to the functioning of the user's device outside the ad by doing things such as installing shortcuts, bookmarks or icons or changing default settings without the user's knowledge and consent. If an ad makes such changes it must be clear to the user which app has made the change and the user must be able to reverse the change easily, by either adjusting the settings on the device, advertising preferences in the app, or uninstalling the app altogether.

Ads must not simulate or impersonate system notifications or warnings.

3. Ad Walls

Forcing the user to click on ads or submit personal information for advertising purposes in order to fully use an app provides a poor user experience and is prohibited. Users must be able to dismiss the ad without penalty.

4. Interfering with Third-party Ads and Websites

Ads associated with your app must not interfere with any ads on a third-party application.

POLICY ENFORCEMENT

In the event that your application is removed from Google Play, you will receive an email notification to that effect. If you have any questions or concerns regarding a removal or a rating/comment from a user, you may contact us at http://support.google.com/googleplay/android-developer. Serious or repeated violations of the Developer Distribution Agreement or this Content Policy will result in account termination. Repeated infringement of intellectual property rights, including copyright, will also result in account termination. For more information on Google's copyright policies, please see here.

Source: © Google, 2012

APPENDIX 5.

BLACKBERRY APP WORLD™ VENDOR GUIDELINES

RIM recognizes that the contributions of application developers are fundamental to the success of the BlackBerry App World™.

The BlackBerry App World™ will strive to deliver the best application discovery experience of high quality offerings for BlackBerry users while simultaneously providing application developers with significant exposure and placement.

RIM shall use the following guidelines when determining whether or not to accept an application submitted by a developer:

• Applications must be the property of and/or validly licensed to the vendor and must not violate intellectual property rights and the inclusion of your applications in the BlackBerry App World™ must not violate any agreements to which you are a party or of which you are otherwise aware;

• Any information shall be true, accurate, current and complete and updated as required. Any information and intellectual property (excluding the applications) that is provided to RIM or its agents as part of or along with an application, including, without limitation, user documentation and marketing materials and trademarks, designs and copyright therein ("Information"), must be the property of and/or validly licensed to the vendor and must not violate intellectual property rights. The inclusion of Information in the BlackBerry App World™ or elsewhere must not violate any agreements to which you are a party or of which you are otherwise aware;

• Applications must be functionally stable in all material respects on the designated target devices and must not interfere with, degrade or adversely affect any software (including, without limitation, other third party applications), service, system, network or data used by any person including RIM or an Airtime Service Provider or otherwise have a detrimental effect upon RIM and/or its brand, an Airtime Service Provider or any of their respective customers or products or services;

• The application must alert users to any potential airtime usage charges, if applicable;

• Applications must not contain or link to any content, or perform any function, that is illegal (e.g. against any criminal, civil or statutory law or regulation), including, without limitation, any libel, obscenity, breach of privacy, infringement or misappropriation of any intellectual property rights and/or other proprietary rights of any third party (including, without limitation, unlawfully circumventing any digital rights management protections), and must not contain or link to any content, or perform any function, that is abusive, belittling, harassing, deceptive, malicious or otherwise inappropriate, or provides for any portion of the suggested retail price to be made available to the end user to risk for possible monetary gain within such application;

• **Applications must be:**
- commercially available;
- designed for installation by end users without further substantial support;
- provided to RIM in object code format only; and
- designed for general end user usage and not designed, developed, customized or modified for a specific customer or end user. Cryptographic functionality in Applications must be limited to the following: authentication, digital signature, or copyright protection. Authentication is defined as access control where there is no encryption of files or text except as directly related to the protection of passwords, Personal Identification Numbers(PINs) or similar data to prevent unauthorized

access. If any cryptographic functionality is contained in any application, such cryptographic functionality cannot be easily changed by the end user;

- **Vendor must:**
- have obtained all necessary permits, licenses, registrations, authorizations, approvals and declarations (including all necessary export permits) for the distribution of the applications and Information to RIM and on or through the BlackBerry App World™; and

- provide RIM with any and all information requested by RIM so that RIM may obtain any necessary permits, licenses, registrations, authorizations, approvals and declarations (including all necessary export permits) to distribute the applications through BlackBerry App World™;

- Applications must be submitted in COD/BAR file format generated using RIM's BlackBerry Java Development Environment (JDE) and/or RIM's JDE Plug-in for Eclipse, and be subject to an agreement relating to the use of those development tools ("BlackBerry SDK Agreement") between RIM and the vendor (or where the vendor is not the original developer of the application, between RIM and the developer);

- Applications and Information must not violate any terms or conditions of the BlackBerry SDK Agreement or any other agreements applicable to the applications or Information. The current version of the BlackBerry SDK Agreement can be found here:http://www.blackberry.com/legal;

- The foregoing points are guidelines only, and RIM reserves the right to accept, deny or remove any application from the BlackBerry App World™ at any time.

Please note that notwithstanding preliminary or final acceptance of an application by RIM for inclusion within the BlackBerry App World™, such application may not be made available in all territories and/or to customers of all airtime service providers due to applicable laws in a specific territory and/or restrictions, including, without limitation, service terms, imposed by the applicable airtime service provider on availability of applications on its network.

Please check back often as updated guidelines may be posted by RIM from time to time.

For further details on the application vetting criteria used to approve applications, please refer to the BlackBerry App World™ Vetting Criteria.

Source:

APPENDIX 6.

APP POLICIES FOR WINDOWS PHONE

To protect the Windows Phone Store service and users of the service, and to address mobile operator requirements, Microsoft has established the following policies for apps offered for distribution in the Windows Phone Store. Microsoft reserves the right to update these policies as needed.

Requirement   Requirement Text

2.1 Your app must be fully functional when acquired from the Windows Phone Store. Unless you have a pre-existing billing relationship with the user, your app may not require the user to provide payment information, within the app experience, to activate, unlock, or extend usage of the app.

2.2 Your app may not sell, link to, or otherwise promote mobile voice plans.

2.3 Your app must not jeopardize the security or functionality of (a) Windows Phone devices or (b) the Windows Phone Store and must not have the potential to cause harm to Windows Phone Users.

2.4 If your app includes or displays advertising, the advertising must comply with the Microsoft Advertising Creative Acceptance Policy Guide and the app must have distinct, substantial and legitimate content and purpose other than the display of advertising.

2.5 If your app requires the download of a large additional data package (e.g. greater than 50 MB) to enable the app to run as described, the app description must disclose the approximate size of the data package and that additional charges may apply depending on connectivity used to acquire data.

2.6 If your app enables chat, instant messaging, or other person-to-person communication and allows the user to setup or create his or her account or ID from the mobile device, the app must include a mechanism to verify that the user creating the account or ID is at least 13 years old.

2.7 The following requirements apply to apps that receive the location of a user's mobile device:

2.7.1 Your app must determine location using the Microsoft Location Service API.

2.7.2 The privacy policy of your app must inform users about how location data from the Location Service API is used and disclosed and the controls that users have over the use and sharing of location data. This can be hosted within or directly linked from the app. The privacy policy must be accessible from your app at any time.

2.7.3 Your app must provide in-app settings that allow the user to enable and disable your app's access to and use of location from the Location Service API.

2.7.4 If your app publishes or makes available location data obtained from the Location Service API to any other service or other person (including advertising networks), your app must implement a method to obtain opt-in consent. To "implement a method to obtain 'opt-in' consent," the app must:
(a) first describe how the location information will be used or shared;

(b) obtain the user's express permission before publishing the location information as described; and

(c) provide a mechanism through which the user can later opt out of having the location information published. Your app must periodically remind users or provide a visual indicator that location data is being sent to any other service or person.

2.7.5 Your app must not override, circumvent, or suppress any Microsoft toast notification or prompts related to the Location Service API.

2.7.6 Your app must not override or circumvent a user's choice to disable location services on the mobile device.

2.7.7 Your app must request location and retain and use location data from the Location Service API only as necessary to deliver the location-aware features your app provides to users.

2.7.8 You and your app must adopt measures to protect against unauthorized access to, use or disclosure of location data received from the Location Service API.

2.8 If your app (a) accesses or uploads a user's Contacts, Photos, Phone number, SMS history, Browsing history or any other data reasonably considered personal in nature, or if your app shares any of the foregoing information with third-party services or individuals, or (b) shares any unique device or user IDs, combined with user information, with third-party services or individuals, the app must implement a method to obtain the user's "opt-in" consent.

To "implement a method to obtain 'opt-in' consent," the app must:
• provide your privacy policy, which at a minimum must describe how the personal information will be accessed, used or shared;

• obtain the user's express permission before accessing, uploading or sharing the information as described; and

• provide a mechanism through which the user can later opt out of having the information accessed, uploaded or shared.

2.9 If your app uses the Microsoft Push Notification Service, the app and the use of the Microsoft Push Notification Service must comply with the following requirements:

2.9.1 The app must first describe the notifications to be provided and obtain the user's express permission (opt-in), and must provide a mechanism through which the user can opt out of receiving push notifications. All notifications provided using the Microsoft Push Notification Service must be consistent with the description provided to the user and must comply with all applicable App policies for Windows Phone, Content policies for Windows Phone andAdditional requirements for specific app types for Windows Phone.

2.9.2 The app and its use of the Microsoft Push Notification Service must not excessively use network capacity or bandwidth of the Microsoft Push Notification Service, or otherwise unduly burden a Windows Phone or other Microsoft device or service with excessive push notifications, as determined by Microsoft in its reasonable discretion, and must not harm or interfere with any Microsoft networks or servers or any third party servers or networks connected to the Microsoft Push Notification Service.

2.9.3 The Microsoft Push Notification Service may not be used to send notifications that are mission critical or otherwise could affect matters of life or death, including without limitation critical notifications related to a medical device or condition. MICROSOFT EXPRESSLY DISCLAIMS ANY WARRANTIES THAT THE USE OF THE MICROSOFT PUSH NOTIFICATION SERVICE OR DELIVERY OF MICROSOFT PUSH

NOTIFICATION SERVICE NOTIFICATIONS WILL BE UNINTERRUPTED, ERROR FREE, OR OTHERWISE GUARANTEED TO OCCUR ON A REAL-TIME BASIS.

2.10 Your app and metadata must have distinct, substantial and legitimate content and purpose. Your app must provide functionality other than launching a webpage and must not be unreasonably priced in relation to the functionality of the app.

2.11 Your app and its associated metadata must accurately represent its functionality, capabilities and features.

2.12 If your app has a Voice Command Definition (VCD) file, the CommandPrefix element in the VCD file and the app name must not be a homophone or an exact match to a speech system command. For a list of speech system commands, see System voice commands for Windows Phone 8. For more information about voice commands, see Voice commands for

WINDOWS PHONE 8:

2.13 The following requirements apply to apps that use in-app purchase:

2.13.1 Your app can sell digital items or services using the in-app purchase API functionality provided by Windows Phone. The in-app item sold in your app must be consumed or used in an app that you develop that runs in a Microsoft platform.

In-app items sold in your app cannot be converted to any legally valid currency (e.g. USD, Euro, etc.), or any physical goods or services, except when using in-app purchase to sell a physical representation of digital content created by the user entirely in a Windows Phone, including photos, music, video text or documents.

You are responsible for delivering the item acquired through in-app purchase.

2.13.2   If your app is offered in Korea, the app description provided during app submission must state that it offers in-app purchase within the app.

2.13.3   You cannot use in-app purchase to sell digital magazines in United States, or any other countries/regions not listed at Tax details for paid apps.

2.13.4   You cannot use in-app purchase to sell VoIP minutes in Australia, Brazil, Turkey or United States.

Source:

APPENDIX 7.

CONTENT POLICIES FOR WINDOWS PHONE

3.1 - Licensed Content, Name, Logo & Trademarks

_____

The following content is allowed where:
• Content and app name are original or licensed.
• Copyrighted content that is used with permission. Use of branded items (logos / trademarks) has been approved by the brand owners.
• If an app depicts any mobile or wired telephone, handheld PDA, or any other data and voice communicator, it must be either generic or a Windows Phone device.
• It is the application provider's responsibility to determine if the app provider has the right to use the chosen name, content, logos, copyright, trademarks, online services & APIs.

3.2 - Illegal or Contemplates Harm

_____

The following content is not allowed:
• Any content that is illegal under applicable local law, obscene, or indecent.
• Any content that depicts or encourages harm or violence against a person or animal in the real world.

3.3 - Defamatory, Libelous, Slanderous, and Threatening

_____

The following content is not allowed:
• Any content that is defamatory, libelous, slanderous, or threatening.
• Any content that facilitates or promotes content prohibited by these guidelines.

3.4 - Hate Speech or Discriminatory

The following content is not allowed:
• Any content that advocates discrimination, hatred, or violence based on considerations of race, ethnicity, national origin, language, gender, age, disability, status as a veteran, religion, sexual orientation or expression, or that promotes organizations devoted to that purpose. Such content can include images or text that perpetuates a negative stereotype of a race, gender, sexual preference or religion. We are particularly inclined to act against content where there is evidence that the intent of posting was to harass, threaten, or insult an individual or group on one of these bases.

3.5 - Alcohol, Tobacco, Weapons, and Drugs

The following content is not allowed:
•   Any content that facilitates or promotes, whether directly or indirectly, the illegal (under applicable local law) or excessive sale or use of alcohol or tobacco products, drugs, or weapons is not allowed on any section/site, regardless of targeting.

3.6 - Adult Related Content

The following content is not allowed:
• Sex / Nudity – Images that are sexually suggestive or provocative (e.g. sexually provocative touching, bondage, masturbation); provocative images that reveal nipples, genitals, buttocks, or pubic hair.
• Content that a reasonable person would consider to be adult or borderline adult content (images, text, video or audio).

- Content that generally falls under the category of pornography.
- Content that depicts or suggests prostitution.
- Content depicting sexual fetishes.
- Content of a sexual nature depicting children or animals.

3.7 - Certain Types of Illegal Activity

The following content is not allowed:
- Any content that facilitates or promotes illegal gambling, illegal adult content and/or pornography, child pornography, bestiality, piracy, illegal online pharmacies, illegal drugs, or criminal or terrorist activities.

- Apps that enable legal gambling in the applicable jurisdiction where legal gambling is allowed may be permitted, subject to the App Provider's acceptance of additional contract terms.

- Any content that instructs users how to make bombs or weapons, drugs, or solicits involvement in behavior that is violent or illegal under applicable local law.

- Unauthorized use of another entity's intellectual property, including but not limited to: software, music, art, and other copyrighted, trademarked or patented materials or trade secrets.

- Any content that facilitates or promotes underage drinking, consumption of illegal drugs, or socially irresponsible behavior due to alcohol or drug consumption (e.g., drinking and driving).

3.8 - Violence

___

The following content is not allowed:

• Realistic or gratuitous violence, including depictions of the following:

- Decapitation, impaling, blood splatter/blood spurting/blood pooling, or gore
- Exploding body parts
- Guns/weapons pointed toward user/audience (e.g., "Russian Roulette" games)
- Strangulation/choking
- People or creatures on fire
- Cruelty to animals
- Audio of humans or animals suffering

• Involuntary or physically-resisted sexual interactions with violent or illicit overtones
• Rape, sexual assault
• Molestation, physical child abuse
• Requests or instructions to injure or otherwise harm a real-world person or group of people
• Glorification of crimes against humanity such as genocide and torture

3.9 - Excessive Profanity

___

The following content is not allowed:
•   Any content with the excessive use of profanity or adult language.

3.10 - Country/Region Specific Requirements

Content that is offensive in any country/region to which your app is targeted is not allowed. Content may be considered offensive in certain countries/regions because of local laws or cultural norms. Examples of potentially offensive content in certain countries/regions include, but are not limited to, the following:

• People in revealing clothing or sexually suggestive poses
• Religious references
• Alcohol references
• Sexual or bathroom humor
• Simulated or actual gambling
• Disputed territory or region references
• Enabling access to content or services that are illegal in the country/region

Countries/regions for which one or more parts of 3.10 may apply include the following:

Group 1: China

Group 2: Albania, Bangladesh, Brunei, Burkina Faso, Chad, Djibouti, Egypt, Indonesia, Jordan, Kazakhstan, Kyrgyzstan, Lebanon, Malaysia, Maldives, Mali, Morocco, Nigeria, Senegal, Sierra Leone, Tajikistan, Tunisia, Turkmenistan, Uzbekistan

Group 3: Afghanistan, Algeria, Azerbaijan, Bahrain, Comoros, Eritrea, Gambia, Guinea, Iraq, Kuwait, Libya, Mauritania, Niger, Oman, Pakistan, Qatar, Saudi Arabia, Somalia, Tanzania, United Arab Emirates, Yemen

3.11 – Game Categorization and Rating Requirements

- Game apps must be categorized as Games.

- Game apps submitted to South Korea, Brazil or Russia markets require a valid game rating certificate.

- Game apps submitted to the Taiwan market must have a rating, and the following warning text must be included in the app description:
earch page results. These should be 70 characters in length, and should offer short descriptions of individual pages they represent, with at least one or two page-relevant keywords within them.

- Image attributes. Images offer excellent SEO-boosting opportunities on Google and other search engines, but it is critical that the photos, graphics, images, etc. have descriptive tags associated with them.

- Internal links. Create a well-organized and thorough link structure within each website page, connecting them to each other through hierarchical text-based hyperlinks.

- External links. Create opportunities for backlinks to your site from other websites so that visitors will be lead back to relevant content on your own website pages. Dedicate time to posting links to social sites, guest post opportunities, articles, blogs, forums, etc., that allow you to publish links back to your website.

- Social media sharing. Install buttons for all the major social sites (Facebook, Twitter, LinkedIn) and other significant platforms on every important page of your website. Readers spread the word,

BLANK WIREFRAME SCREENS

AT&T 1:09 PM 97%

AT&T 1:09 PM 97%

APPENDIX 8

APPENDIX 8

APPENDIX 8

APPENDIX 8

APPENDIX 8

APPENDIX 8

APPENDIX 8

APPENDIX 8

APPENDIX 8